Observations of
A Pilgrim

Observations of
A Pilgrim

By
Michael Grebe

Edited by
Richard L. Harvel

To order additional copies of this book, contact:
Xlibris Corporation
1-888-795-4274
www.Xlibris.com
Orders@Xlibris.com
121589

Contents

Acknowledgements

I would be remiss if I did not thank my wife Mary for her support and patience with me during the days, weeks, and months of producing this work.

Also I must acknowledge the influence and support of my very dear friend Richard L. Harvel, for without his encouragement I might never have attempted to publish this, "work of love". His belief that many people might enjoy this work pushed me to carry out this task to the finish.

Lastly; I must above all else praise, and thank my savior for God's intervention in my life. I had no idea why God placed these poems in my mind, nor why I began to put them to paper. It was only as I shared what God was doing in my life that the encouragement to produce this book, of what God had laid on my heart, began to give me faith that others might find inspiration, solace, and hope from my feeble and inexperienced attempts to express insights God had shared with me. I pray some soul might find a new inspiration and a vision of God's love for the world and especially for himself.

Observations of a Pilgrim

A lad of nine, an empty room,
    a simple folding chair,
Alone with God, he faced his need,
    and met the savior there.
It was not chance that set the stage,
    no accident of fate.
A troubled child, the loving Lord,
    a journey through the gate,
Where hidden sin was brought to light,
    his guilt so clearly seen.
Forgiveness calmed a troubled soul,
    and washed it pure and clean.
This is no tale contrived to stir
    the hearts of men like we.
It is the truth, it is the way,
    that God reached out to me!

At the age of nine I received my first copy of God's Word. It was a small green New Testament with the Psalms. I began to read it, and over the period of several months I had read through The Gospel of Matthew and most of the Gospel of Mark.

Ours was a large family with eight children. Our transportation was provided by a 1936 Plymouth two door sedan. It was extremely difficult to cram ten people into that small vehicle. A revival had begun at a church in town. My father, mother, three older brothers, and older sister, all gave their hearts to God during the week day services. I had been left at home those nights allowing the older children to attend the services. Sunday morning I was allowed to attend the services. When the Sunday School dismissed, before I left the room, I knelt beside my small folding chair and prayed. I asked for forgiveness for my sins and accepted Jesus as my savior. No one witnessed my conversion except God the father, Son, Holy Spirit, and the heavenly angels. When I left that basement Sunday school room I knew beyond all doubt that I had given myself to God, and He had accepted me as his child. That scene took place in the fall of 1949. After my seventieth birthday, in 2010 I was inspired to put to paper my testimony. My Journey was the product of that inspiration; it became the inspiration for the work that followed. I have named the product of that inspiration; "Observations of a Pilgrim". The sixty one years that have transpired following my conversion, is the background that God has used to help me put to paper this collection of poetry. I hope you find something that might inspire you as you read what God has drawn forth from my heart and experiences.

The Journey

My threescore and ten have swiftly passed by,
    the days of my youth are no more.
The pathways I roamed seem rougher and steeper
    the light not so bright as before.
Yes the summer's far spent, the harvest's most in,
    the path's end now calls me on high,
A vision I see of my heavenly home
    and my heart hears encouraging cries.
I almost can see through the gates made of pearl,
    my treasures laid by there in store,
Many friends and loved ones are cheering me on,
    down the path they have taken before.
As I focus on Christ, earth's treasures grow dim,
    they no longer appeal to my eye.
There are steps yet before me, I must needs carry on,
    till I gain that home past the sky.
The weaker I am, the stronger he grows,
    this world's trinkets now all laid aside,
To Christ's hand I now more tightly cling,
    'neath his healing wings I abide.
I still feel the call he laid on my heart
    in the clouds of my life's distant past.
I often failed him, he never failed me,
    his grace more than my heart could ask.
He has carried me on, through all of my days,
    no greater friend ever I've known.
My dwelling he's preparing, his presence I'm sharing,
    I admit, I yearn to go home!

I feel compelled to share these simple truths. I confess that God is the author and originator of all contained in these pages. I pray that you the reader might share the vision.

One

I found myself no more or less,
    a son of Adam's race.
I'd be like God, by my own hands,
    and proudly take my place.
I had my pride, I knew my mind,
    I'd stand by my own ends,
And my mistake so certain was,
    that Jesus' blood would cleanse.
My thoughts and goals so lofty were,
    I knew God would approve,
And by my words and by my deeds,
    the world would surely move.
But crumbled and ruined around me lay,
    my work . . . not one thing stood.
The edifice of stone I sought to build,
    contained just rotten wood.
If God builds not the house,
    the scripture doth proclaim,
"The workman works, but all his toil,
    is found to be in vain."
With tears of guilt, my soul cried out,
    with head bowed low in shame,
"Lord help me stand, but in your strength,
    and then I might attain."

The tendency of the human Spirit to depend on one's strength and wisdom often leads us to attempt, as Adam tried, to achieve god-like status by our own efforts.

Lord strip us of our arrogant attitude of telling you to carry out that which we think you need to do in our lives and your world.

Two

"This is the day the Lord has made",
    my heart can joyfully sing,
While gentle breezes softly blow,
    and cheerful birdsong rings.
But what of days when storm clouds race,
    with lightning across the sky,
When darkness seeks to hide the soul,
    and tears would dim the eye?
Have we not learned the simple truth,
    spelled out by God so clear,
That God can turn all things to good,
    for those who trust him here?
Shall I demand just pleasant days,
    on me his blessings pour?
For 'tis in dungeons, dark and deep,
    I need him all the more.
It takes no faith to walk smooth paths
    when things are going fine,
But sweeter still, the promise made;
    "my child you know you're mine."
The Word declares, there is no place,
    where I can hide from thee,
No matter where I find myself,
    there shall your presence be.
This is the day, the Lord has made,
    let me rejoice and sing,
And walk in faith, to trust my God,
    to watch o'er everything.

Many today seek to have us believe God allows only pleasant paths and material abundance to come to his children; Ignoring those who suffered great trials and were called; "those of whom the world was not worthy." Job and others prove God keeps us secure in the midst of trials and gives us peace that the world can never know!

Three

How anxious does the heart become,
    when faced with the unknown?
The urge to act more swiftly then
    is not my thought alone.
When chaos, turmoil, frantic deeds,
    and tumults fills one's life,
Our feeble struggles from within,
    adds only to the strife.
Elijah alone in deep despair,
    stood thinking all was lost,
While quakes and wind, yes even fire,
    before his vision crossed;
But when the frenzy all had ceased,
    a still small voice was heard.
Then calm and peace and confidence,
    upon his soul conferred.
Why should we all so weak and frail,
    fight helpless o'er our plight,
When we could stand in victory,
    secure in God's own might?

"Be still and know that I am God:" is the message seldom heard by the inhabitants of this world. We break ourselves upon barriers that stand resolute in our way, when we could step aside and allow The Almighty God to open the path before us. Never forget that God alone can part the waters. Our job is to walk across on the dry land He has provided for us.

Four

I am persuaded, my heart agrees,
    eternal words ring true.
No circumstance or trial sore,
    can keep my heart from you.
God is the anchor of my soul,
    my hope for days to come;
When time stands still and tried by fire,
    'twill be what he has done.
No noble, marble monuments,
    or gallant deeds we'll claim.
He's able to keep, which I've committed,
    eternal to his name.
I seek no grand or hallowed hall
    in honor built for me;
"Well done thou good and faithful steward;"
    I fain would hear from thee.

As I look back on the journey I have undertaken, I find the only time I made worthwhile progress was when I was led by the hand of God! I have come to realize; success is not measured by the volume of our achievements, but rather in the quality. It seems too often we would fill the day with activity when we would better serve God by heeding his call to; "come ye aside for a season," and quietly dwell in the holy presence of our God, allowing him to control the emphasis of the day, and the direction of our life.

Five

Ah Lord; "I am but a mere child;"
    I hear the prophet cry.
"Thus why should you begin this task,
    with such a one as I?
A nameless face in any crowd:
    unknown, unsung, unheard.
Who would listen, should I dare speak?"
    The thought to me absurd.
A still small voice within the soul,
    a tug upon the heart
Bade me go on, to lift my voice;
    demands of me my part.
The race is not unto the swift,
    nor battle to the strong,
The power of God will win the day.
    Lift high the voice in song.
He traps the wise with foolishness,
    man's wisdom only fails,
And by the weak things of this earth,
    God's purpose yet prevails.
When we shall lose our lives in him,
    our life may then begin,
And when that final trump shall sound,
    triumphant we shall win.

The Christian empowered by God will always prove to be the winning combination in any battle of life. We must acknowledge our utter lack of sufficient strength before God will empower us; remember the words, "not by power nor by might, but by my Spirit sayeth the Lord."

Six

I come to God with simple plea;
"Oh Lord, please take this thorn from me.
What deeds my hands might then bring forth,
all for your cause upon this earth?"

"My heart can dream of greater things,
which all to you I'd gladly bring."
His answer came, "Come learn of me,
to reach such heights go to your knees."

"The strength required to meet my call,
can never come from man at all.
The clay must yield to potter's hand,
if you, my vessel, wish to stand."

"The will of man must broken be,
ere I, can use that man for me.
That thorn you beg me to displace,
o're it you'll find sufficient grace."

Man with pride yet still goes forth,
but humbled, prostrate finds his worth.
So ask not from your thorn to flee,
just seek that grace reserved for thee!

    The wisdom of God that assures us victory, seems foolish to the natural heart, but the circumstances of life that would mold us into the individual God can use, will always take us to the point of admitting, "I can go no farther unless God leads." It seems that we humans need to be reminded over and over, "The battle is the Lords."

Seven

Thy word have I hid in my heart,
    that I might not sin against thee,
A purpose divine, a promise of faith,
    a pledge of my heart given free,
For I cannot see through the mists of this life,
    the path lies uncertain to me.
Thus I trust to my guide to lead safely on,
    convinced of the end he can see.
Years I traveled a path, one of my choice,
    found nothing of worth there for me,
The guilt and the shame, the shackles of sin,
    out of fear I thought but to flee.
But never a place where my heart felt at ease;
    not a shelter or haven could see.
But when at the cross, I confessed all my sin,
    forgiveness and peace came to me.
I shall never turn back to the things of this world,
    sin's guilt and pain I shall flee.
God's Word have I hidden, deep in my heart,
    encircled in love I'm now free.

David testified to hiding God's word in his heart to avoid displeasing his Lord. If we desire to live an overcoming, victorious life, we need to walk close to Jesus. The apostle John in his gospel begins with, "In the beginning was the Word, the Word was with God, and the Word was God—The Word became flesh and dwelt among us." The only way we can know Jesus, is to know the Word. Christ is the eternal Word. When we decide the Bible is more than a reading book and begin to study, really study it, then we will truly find the eternal Christ; the friend that sticketh closer than a brother.

Eight

I entered this world with nothing to claim,
    helpless and needy 'tis true.
Jesus said come, "as a little child,"
    but with pride it's a hard thing to do.
We find it hard to admit to our selves,
    there is nothing to Christ we might bring.
He is the very air that I breathe,
    then to what of my own may I cling?
What is the thing I brought to this world,
    with what shall I leave when I go?
Man faced by God, and his claim on our lives;
    how often an arrogant "No"?
To take one's own naked bare hands,
    to dig down a mountain of stone,
What utter folly, what man with right mind,
    would make such a project his own?
And yet filled with pride and stubborn resolve,
    we assume our God to command;
"I'll work my way to that heavenly place,
    I'll make it by my own two hands!"
If I should desire a gain from this life,
    like an infant my needs I must lay,
With true humble heart at Jesus' own feet,
    requesting his strength for my days.
We can find strength, our weakness confessed,
    his grace is sufficient for all,
Victorious on earth, Satan's hoards put to flight,
    our goal, to enter God's hall.

So many people hope to earn God's love, assuming they might win his approval by their actions. Not until we admit that our only hope lies in God's love and forgiveness through Christ's death and resurrection, will we find peace in this world and the one to come.

Nine

A field and a planter;
  good soil and good seed;
But with the wheat's blade,
  whence cometh the weed?
The world is the seedbed,
  where both would fain grow,
Oh let us beware,
  of what Satan might sow.
Let us not be weary,
  and sleep in the night,
To be shamed at the harvest,
  with a reaping too light.
My brother's keeper,
  that task have I shunned?
Each man is my neighbor?
  My duty I've done?
Oh bring them to Jesus,
  their souls to renew.
Our job is to bring them,
  whether many or few.
God grant me a vision,
  of a field harvest white,
And send me to harvest,
  to reap all in sight.

Jesus' command, to go into all the world and make disciples, has echoed down through the ages to every born again child of God. The field belongs to the master, it is our job to occupy and harvest that field. Dare I attempt to stand at the judgment throne unashamed with empty hands?

Ten

In the mists of time and ages long past,
    the heroic deeds of great men,
Are often applauded and held for review
    with no thought for the circumstance then.
We read of a mother and the love of her child;
    the hope of her nation—her dream.
The rushes she wove, and the babe that she hid,
    in the reeds of the Nile's muddy stream.
The babe he then grew and time swiftly passed,
    he was destined to be a great man.
But position and rank could not fill the place,
    was not part of God's master plan.
A man and a dream, a common grave shared,
    neath the desert's dry shifting sands.
A broken deliverer fled for his life
    to a barren and harsh distant land.
How different the scene, the man we now find,
    keeping watch o'er another man's flocks.
Four score years have passed, what can he claim,
    some sheep, some bushes, and rocks?
But there on the mount, in the desert that day,
    a bush burned, but was not consumed.
And there on the mount, in the desert that day,
    his life's great calling resumed.
So when you are distressed at the time that's far spent,
    don't fret, don't worry or push.
Or you might miss the place of God's Holy Ground
    and the timing of God's burning bush.
Never let it be said that you've failed in your life,
    as long as God gives you breath,
For life's not restricted, to this shell of clay,
    nor can it be silenced by death.

We read in the Word, of stewards once charged,
    with tasks, both great and small
When the master returned, and settled accounts,
    there was still obligations for all.
So let the Lord lead and don't run ahead,
    don't fret, don't worry, or push.
Or you might miss the place, of God's Holy Ground
    and the timing of your burning bush.

Eleven

Where hath it gone, that filled the soul,
That lifted up an honored goal,
The heart that yearned for those nearby,
The tears that fall when strong men cry?

It seems that, when I look around,
Sin and vanity abound.
Compassion all has fled this earth,
Left mankind's souls in deepest dearth.

The masses all in deep despair,
They cry aloud, they beat the air.
And yet we turn our eyes away,
Continue in our worthless play,

Of acting good and speaking bold,
Yet all the while our hearts are cold.
God grant we all with bitter cry,
Call out, "Christ. we die we die."

Oh help us Lord, to rise again,
Convict the world, of God and sin.
Till all around us we shall see,
Those sin sick souls, bowed down to thee.
We shall see this thing perhaps,
If we make up the hedge and stand in the gaps.

The attitude of the average Christian today seems to be that of seeking only to escape hell. If that is our response to God's calling, then we are only looking for a "fire escape," for our souls. There is no peace or joy in such a response to God. Let us all strive for a better relationship with our creator. A relationship of love and commitment that brings peace, joy and closeness only found in total dedication to Christ.

Twelve

A child's faith can reach,
　　what the mind cannot hold,
And humbly walk out,
　　to be ever so bold.
While those known for wisdom,
　　cannot comprehend,
Nor grasp in their power,
　　the message God sends.
Caught up in their vision,
　　and lost in their pride,
The simple and humble,
　　their minds can't abide.
But truth is not measured,
　　by mere mortal thought,
And grace can't be bartered,
　　nor can it be bought.
This world's greatest treasures,
　　so seldom they find,
Aren't locked in the storehouse,
　　of mere mortal minds.
The plain and the simple,
　　confounding the wise,
Points out all the follies,
　　unperceived by their eyes,
For God isn't conquered,
　　nor is he impressed,
By worldly opinions,
　　the masses have stressed.
He seeks no approval,
　　nor considers their ways,
He's alpha omega,
　　the ancient of days.

The day is coming when the pompous, arrogant, self impressed people of this world will realize; simple faith in God, is the only wise choice in this life!

Thirteen

Forsake not assembling, sounds deep in my heart,
    my mind echoes back "amen".
Nothing's so sweet, as the fellowship found,
    in the family of God; my friends.
My daily walk, midst this sinful world,
    it fain would tatter my soul.
When welcomed by saints and stirred by great hymns,
    I focus on eternal goals.
In the cool of the evening, Adam walked with his God,
    fellowship, oh so sublime.
Though the garden be gone, I rejoice in the song,
    "Blessed be the tie that binds."
I need every day, the strength I receive,
    from his presence, midst others like me,
And closer I come to my loving Lord,
    in the midst of worship so free.
I love the Church, the pure bride of Christ,
    she awaits the bridegroom's last call,
She is the temple of God on this earth,
    his mercy and grace there for all.
How hollow the words uttered by men,
    excusing their turning away.
All must face the truth, we each made our choice,
    no one stood in our way.
We can't lay the blame for holding aloof,
    on some poor example we see.
We are, who we are, by decisions *we made.*
    No one made decisions for thee.

We have all heard some child exclaim, "look what you made me do." It is time to own up to our own responsibility for the choices we have made. Some wise man remarked , "You have to be smaller than a hypocrite to hide behind him!"

Fourteen

I stand amazed with humbled heart,
    when faced with all I see:
A tiny bloom, a blade of grass,
    a mountain's dignity.
All the beauty of this earth,
    shouts forth it's praise of God.
What of the one, whose blinded eye,
    sees naught upon this sod,
Who casts his gaze, with empty heart,
    on all the eye can see,
To turn his back, and close his mind,
    in his impunity,
And think to stand, by his own strength,
    sufficient on his own.
But he shall fail, all crushed to earth,
    ere half the gale has blown.
One grain of sand, more strength contains,
    to stop the swelling tide,
Than all the strength, man calls his own,
    deceived by his own pride.
"Greater deeds, than I have done",
    the promise of my King.
This strength to me he will bestow,
    if I give everything.

Little is much if God is in it, is a truth as old as time. This source of power is so often rejected, and denied by those who would exclude God from the scene. Their pride will not allow them to take second place to God, and so doing they deny themselves access to the greatest power on earth.

Fifteen

There is a title, so often used,
    so loosely tossed about,
So misconstrued with no concept
    of what that name doth shout.
They first called them "Christians",
    back then in Antioch.
Were we required their sacrifice,
    would we dare join their flock?
How many now would fall away,
    deny the cause they claim,
And slink away to hide the face,
    ashamed of Jesus' name?
We live in ease and luxury,
    a race of pampered souls.
We ask no pain be placed on us,
    no price to reach the goal.
We hope to move, unscathed in life:
    just walk through Heaven's gate,
And many choose to use Christ's name,
    to circumvent their fate.
Repent, turn back, yes, bow the knee,
    confess to God your sin,
Look up in faith, take up your cross,
    And, yes, be born again.
Not every one who cries "Lord, Lord"
    escapes hell's fiery flood,
'Tis only those who heed the call,
    those washed in Jesus' blood.

Claiming Christ's name is meaningless without first accepting his claim upon our lives. It behooves us all to establish our birthright through God's grace before we can expect to reap the privileges of family membership.

Sixteen

The people perish, where no vision is;
    the Bible clearly states.
Can I today, complacent be,
    ignoring mankind's fate?
He calls us now, our station to be,
    a watchman upon the wall,
To lift the voice, to warn all men,
    reveal to them God's call.
Oh God, we need a vision clear,
    your burden fill our heart,
Wake us from sleep and slumber now,
    your mission, help us start.
Our enemy, the destroyer of souls,
    even now assails the gate.
People of God, shake off your sloth,
    there is no time to wait.
How can I now just rest secure,
    inside salvations walls?
The battle for souls is raging *now;*
    our foes from hell's own halls,
If one should fail, within my reach,
    not told, of God's good grace,
How might I stand and face my God,
    if I fill not my place?

How common today to find professed Christians who carry no burden for the lost souls all around them. May God condemn our hearts, if we do not rise to the task of being a watchman for souls. Oh God help us to realize that the battle for souls is raging all around us, help us to be effective today.

Seventeen

"Eye hath not seen"; the writer once penned,
    of a home we seek to receive.
No reward for deeds done in this life,
    'twill be ours, because we believe.
I fain would seek honor, bring glory to him,
    my trophies to lay at his throne.
But naught could I claim of my meager store,
    on this earth, nothing is my own.
My entry assured by blood that was spilled,
    on Golgotha, by God's only Son.
"It is finished", he cried, while upon that old cross,
    and there my pardon was won.
I can't fathom why he died for my sake;
    'twas my sin, caused Jesus to bleed.
Forever a debtor, I'll walk in his steps,
    where ever his pathway might lead.
Not one of this earth shall yet ever claim,
    to be worthy of what lies in store.
The sacrifice made, by Jesus, God's Son,
    was sufficient for sin, and yes more.
By his Word and his love, his mercy and grace,
    the journey unknown, lies ahead.
I'll not question the way, nor shun the path,
    untill by him into Heaven I'm lead.

It is pride that drives the human mind, to seek to earn God's favor. Falling on one's knees admitting that without Christ, we are nothing but failures, brings us to the point where we can be victorious.

The old song, "Jesus Keep Me Near The Cross" reminds us to keep our perspective centered on the cross and our savior.

Eighteen

Memories of deeds recalled from our past,
    Satan sends to trouble our souls,
Hindering our footsteps along life's way,
    often obscuring our goals.
Raising up sorrows deep in the heart,
    with questions that trouble the mind.
Stirring up fears that our past mistakes
    haven't been all left behind.
When we lay at the feet of our blessed Lord,
    the error of our sinful past,
Into the sea, remembered no more,
    all our guilt forever is cast.
Today by faith with heads lifted up,
    step out with hearts now made free,
Knowing that God forgives all I've done,
    let it not again trouble me.
Help me to grow where I can look back,
    unhindered by deeds of the past,
And just see the grace and love of my Lord,
    and his forgiveness that lasts.

Often times we Christians feel the shame of past sins so strongly that we fail to forgive ourselves for past deeds. Such action restricts the possibilities of our growing in grace, or reaching our full potential for God. We should not refuse to acknowledge our misdeeds, but when God forgives us of them, we need to allow that forgiveness to move them out of our pathway and make it possible to grow beyond them.

Nineteen

I dare not claim a vision mine,
    God's Spirit brings to me.
There is no merit within myself,
    if I would his vessel be.
All praise and honor be now to God,
    the vessel only stows,
And pouring out God's wondrous grace
    is how his kingdom grows.
I cannot hoard unto myself,
    the blessed gifts of grace,
Freely received and freely shared,
    with all of Adam's race.
I ask not for a pleasant path,
    to lead me to my post.
The darkest corners of this earth,
    are where he's needed most.
Redeeming love I needs must share,
    I cannot choose the place
Or path my feet shall travel down,
    If I would spread his grace.
Only a servant upon this earth,
    he measures out my days.
I only hope to hear these words,
    "My child, you've walked my ways.
Come enter now into the place
    I have reserved for thee,
Where peace, and Joy, and blessedness,
    be yours eternally."

"The race is not to the swift, nor the battle to the strong!" Had I known before hand what troubles lay ahead of me, I might have given up in despair, before I started. My Lord has walked the path before me and granted sufficient grace to sustain my every step.

Twenty

"I deserve more!" this claim often heard,
    from the tongues of so many men,
I stand amazed, I ask in my heart,
    "Just why, just where, and just when?"
Today the one who shouts such a cry,
    like Adam's when facing the tree,
Seeks to stand, equal with God,
    with wisdom and knowledge as he.
No one ever has and none ever will,
    find a path that leads to such heights.
Created we are, created remain,
    yet prideful, demanding our rights.
The potter shall always hold o'er the clay,
    the power to shape as he will.
The vessel he makes has a purpose on earth,
    the choice is God's how to fill.
We can break ourselves on eternal rock,
    or accept the calling he gives,
To be cast aside in the refuse of life,
    or dwell in God's purpose and live.

A well known singer was known by a song he often sang. He considered it his trademark. "I did it my way" I wonder what God's response will be if that man stands before the judgment bar, and boasts "I did it my way."

If ever an epithet be placed upon a stone in my memory, let it say "I did it thy way."

Twenty One

How often has man stood at some point
    and dreamed a dream oh so grand,
Swelling with pride, strode forth to the task,
    content in the strength of his hands?
"I'll bend and I'll shape this earth to my mold,
    I'll prove by what my hand brings",
The toil, sweat and tears of spending himself,
    till at last to one breath he clings.
He turns to look back at the sum of his life,
    from a new perspective he's gained,
A vision of all the work of his hands,
    the monument for which his life drained.
His days and his youth, his dreams and his plans,
    the struggle at last to the fore,
Brought to focus by a vision of what lay behind,
    and what lay at eternity's door.
The castles and kingdoms, the greatness of deeds,
    the sum of one mortal life,
Lay in shambles and rags, littered and strewn,
    over a field marked only by strife,
Of efforts to shape, to form of this earth,
    an example of great human deeds,
Bereft of all pride with no place to hide,
    before God, he could now see his need.

Too often, it has been too late, that we human beings realize the awesomeness of our creator. Let none of us think we have nothing in common with the life pictured above.

Twenty Two

Dust of this earth, an almighty hand,
    the spoken Word went forth.
A simple form, by breath of life,
    became a thing of worth.
To call a royal king abroad,
    to tread a dusty road,
To die in shame upon a cross,
    to lift the creature's load.
Could love divine ever speak so loud,
    as then upon that day,
When man's creator took up a cross,
    for just a piece of clay?
My mind can never comprehend
    why such should come to pass.
I stand in awe, I have no words,
    my look is downward cast.
Who am I, amid all this scheme,
    of time and things arrayed?
The object of such matchless love,
    from one whom I betrayed.
Somewhere within the eye of God,
    a greater worth must see.
Should He devote that sacred head,
    for such a lot as we.
The wisdom of the Son of God,
    to act as he doth deign,
Must point to truth beyond our ken,
    thus we must let him reign.

I cannot question the wisdom, mercy, grace, and love of our God, who proposed a plan demanding the life of his Son to redeem the souls of his creation! I can only accept it!

Twenty Three

At times I sit amazed and watch
    as words break forth, so plain,
And seem to know the breath of God,
    'tis nothing I can claim.
But he would use a shell of clay,
    if we would empty be,
And fill us up till we over flow,
    with living water free.
So I shall offer all I am,
    a channel for his love.
Mayhap a thirsting, weary soul,
    to point to God above.
The vessel adds not of itself,
    to that contained within.
It only holds and then pours forth,
    at times approved by him.
"Oh help me, God, let not one whit,
    of who, or what I be,
Flow out upon some soul or heart,
    now searching, Lord, for thee.
Just keep me, fill me, place me Lord
    in some convenient place.
Let everyone who looks on me,
    see just your loving face."

If Christians projected only Christ, what would be the result in our everyday world? Can you imagine the effect and impact the church could make if others only saw Christ in those of us who claim Jesus?

Twenty Four

Never a heart ache, a pain, or a tear,
    fell unnoticed, unfelt to this earth.
To look upon Christ and his sacrifice,
    should teach us what one soul is worth.
We see a woman, both scorned and shamed,
    as she wept at our master's feet.
She washed with her tears, dried with her hair,
    and anointed with oil complete.
The host of the house drew his righteous robes
    about him in utter dismay.
Said to himself, his guest should be shamed,
    to be touched by one of her way.
One woman's guilt, laid at God's feet,
    repentant o'er a life once brought low.
Where much is forgiven, much more on the heart,
    of his love the master bestows.
How different, how strange, the people involved,
    in a scene from reality bare,
The haughty proud host, the woman of shame,
    both caught in a lesson so rare.
Both needed the gift of forgiveness and love,
    both needed a touch from the king,
But only one found the answer that night,
    'twas the answer repentance can bring.
If we would be wise, and learn from this scene,
    the message for all there to see,
Before I look at the guilt in another's life,
    I must first take a good look at me.

"I" trouble seems to plague our society and has done so ever since the Garden of Eden. "I would be like God, and know good and evil;" "I want to do it myself." "I am not like, that publican over there." If you want help with your "I" trouble try these words; "I am crucified with Christ."

Twenty Five

A vision unfolds, unshackled by time,
　　fills the mind with grace all unseen,
A glimpse of a heart, the shade of God's love,
　　impressions so clear and so keen.
It flows like a dream, softly spun in the night,
　　out of reach and yet ever so near.
To rise like the mist over a meadow in spring,
　　it's a song not heard by the ear.
As the stars standing out in a cold winter sky,
　　a message not written by hand,
A symphony heard, deeply stirring the heart,
　　flowing down from a heavenly land.
The skeptic would cry; "It cannot be real,
　　it's nothing my finger might touch.
I must feel its form, weigh it on my scale,
　　give me proof my hands can clutch."
How do we weigh the trust of a babe,
　　nestled close to a mother's warm breast?
With what do we measure the force of a love,
　　bringing peace and solace and rest?
Can we weigh thoughts, touch with our hands,
　　the contents of our finite mind?
How dare we demand God bow to our will
　　and prove he is truly divine?

Any person who claims he does not practice faith is a liar. We exercise faith practically every moment of our lives and think nothing of it. We expect the next breath we take to contain enough oxygen to sustain us. We expect our car to start when we turn the ignition on. We expect this world to be here while we formulate our plans for the future. It is rebellious pride that demands God to prove himself to us. Let the skeptic prove God does not exist!

Twenty Six

A crowded inn, a man and maid,
    a stable dark and cold.
A new born son, now laid to rest,
    a promise made of old.
A virgin's son of humble birth,
    his title, "King of kings."
A group of shepherds in the fields,
    a song that angels sing.
A tiresome trek, a star to guide,
    a humble village scene,
Wise men seeking for the child,
    revealed by vision keen.
Yet over it all, of hope's grand dream,
    a darkened shadow tossed,
Of death and pain and suffering,
    a cruel and rugged cross.
A howling mob with curse and scream,
    "Away, be done with him."
A lifeless body borne in haste,
    midst evening's shadows dim.
Wept and mourned by those he loved,
    laid in a borrowed grave,
The pure and sinless Son of God,
    his life he freely gave.
And I could cast my hope away,
    distressed 'neath Calvary's gloom,
Had I not walked that garden path,
    and seen the empty tomb.

Hell expended all of its power hoping to destroy the work of Christ, but only enabled the fulfillment of God's plan of salvation through the death of Christ. Jesus forced death to take hold of Him and by rising from the grave, defeated death forever. Truly He is the first fruits of the resurrection, and we shall follow.

Twenty Seven

The reasoning mind of mortal man,
　　would cast away God's plan,
While knowing not he is a slave,
　　a pawn in Satan's hand.
The wisdom of this present world,
　　enslaves his heart and soul.
It leads to folly, imagined truth,
　　and hollow mocking goals.
How sad the fate of blinded eyes,
　　of those who claim to see,
They struggle, fall and fail to rise,
　　from pits of sophistry.
The pride filled egos of such men
　　claim freedom for the mind.
The sad results of ruined lives
　　leaves naught of worth behind.
The wasted carnage scattered round,
　　claimed messengers of light.
The empty husks of souls destroyed,
　　the fruit of Satan's blight.
If one might speak with humble heart,
　　that one to God could flee,
Confess the need, repent the path,
　　and rest that soul in thee.

Someone once stated; "The road to hell, is paved with good intentions." That might be so, but the road bed is surely plowed and made ready by human pride. It is certain that the most incorrigible aspect of the human soul is it's refusal to admit; "I was wrong." To their thinking it would bring shame upon them.

Twenty Eight

Someone described the soul of man,
    akin to parchment bare.
It starts unstained and then, the deeds
    of life are written there.
Be all this true, is there a man
    prepared to take his place,
To stand unbowed and unashamed,
    before his makers face?
Could we find one who dares to read
    the ledger of his years,
To face the balance on the page,
    his heart all free from fear?
All we must give account to God,
    as each placed in this land,
But not a one of Adam's race
    Can claim pure heart and hands.
The curse that fell in Eden fair,
    when parents chose to eat,
Thus now we find within the heart,
    the law of straying feet.
But love won out, God had a plan,
    before he shaped the clay,
To send his Son, the sacrifice,
    to lift our guilt away.
Now each must take, that step alone,
    should we desire to live,
To bring to him our *sacrifice*
    of heart and will, to give.
And thus inscribed upon our souls
    a record all might see.
Written in blood, "I claim this one,
    this child belongs to me."

We, who have been dead to God by our sin, can obtain life through Christ's death and resurrection. We can be, "new creatures in Christ." Thanks to our *"Living Lord"*

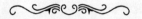

Twenty Nine

In the beginning, the Word went forth
    and all before You lay,
Worlds and stars and universe,
    a shapeless mass of clay.
You breathed in man the breath of life,
    Your image we received.
But, when faced with simple test,
    the serpent's tale believed.
The trees, the rocks, the mountains high,
    cannot but sing Thy praise.
They always have and always will,
    be that for which they're raised.
The man was placed upon this earth,
    with greater, higher goals.
Lower than the angels here,
    with hearts and minds and souls.
You placed Adam and his mate
    in Eden's blessed store,
And only banned to him one tree
    and asked for nothing more.
Its fruit designed to test the will,
    to listen and obey,
To live in trust and pleasantness,
    or cast it all away.
What might have been, had Adam stood
    the test that fateful day?
Transformed, to rise, for all mankind;
    but we remain of clay.

Someone remarked, "the saddest phrase of tongue or pen; the simple words; it might have been." Each of us need to acknowledge that we, like Adam, have walked in our own ways, and are guilty of the same sin that Adam committed; We want to be like God. We want to have our own way. We cannot place the blame for our sin at Adam's feet.

Thirty

The human mind so often soars,
    inspired by visions brave,
To join the masses, blindly led,
    like lemmings to the grave.
The herd instinct can grip one's soul,
    to act without a thought,
And rush unseeing o'er the brink,
    to destinies unsought.
To act in haste may lead the soul
    to endless heart's regret.
The means required to meet the ends,
    in heartache it begets,
A brood of shame and sorrow's deeds,
    the legacy of tears.
'Twill bide it's time, and lull us on,
    unseen throughout the years.
And when our force and youth is spent,
    it then will rear it's head,
To mock and gloat, o'er misspent days,
    the path where we were led.
But we can find the greater good,
    the path that leads to life,
To reach the hand and lift the heart,
    while still beset by strife.
For there is yet the Spirit's call,
    for all who walk this sod,
And each of us, and every day,
    can know the love of God.

While still a youth, God impressed upon my heart; *"The Christian's duty is not to choose between good and evil; rather it is to choose between the good and the best!* It is possible to spend a life doing good, yet totally miss God's calling for your life.

Thirty One

Our Lord shared a story of a field and some seed,
    the story speaks of the heart.
The seed all the same, the difference it seems,
    was the soil; how it played it's part.
God's Word is a seed that only takes root
    in the soil of a heart, where it's sown,
But the soil's condition is left to each man,
    the preparation of each is his own.
The seed always grows when the soil is right,
    what it bears is due to just one,
And the harvest will tell the work of the heart,
    when all of the reaping is done.
So don't blame the seed and don't blame the world,
    if what you reap is too few,
For all had the soil, and all had the seed,
    the preparation was left up to you.

Rarely does one find a person who is willing to accept the blame for the results of a life that has failed to live up its expectations. The fact remains that God gives each man or woman a chance to be all he or she might be.

Just remember this one thing, God does not judge by rules established by mankind's opinion. Jesus commended the widow for giving her two mites, saying she had given more than all the others combined. The depth of our devotion to God is not measured on human scales.

Thirty Two

One man and one woman, a garden's delights,
    provided in beauty so fair,
To walk in the presence of almighty God
    each day in the evening's cool air.
One simple command, a test of their love,
    one tree from the fruit to refrain,
One simple act to taste of the fruit,
    the heart's deepest sorrow had gained.
Now hiding in shame, aware of their loss,
    and seeking some other to blame.
Of evil and good they now understood,
    the price was paid out in their shame.
What price on the heart of a kind loving God
    would he now willingly pay,
To bring back to him the family of man,
    like sheep who had wandered away?
Justice demanded sin's payment in full,
    by the blood of a pure sacrifice.
Not a man could be found unspotted from sin,
    not one worthy the price.
The Spirit of God overshadowed a maid,
    who willingly bore God a Son,
Who took on himself all the sin and the guilt
    that justice might fully be done.
The punishment due for each act of sin,
    completely and totally paid,
That man once again might walk with his God,
    in Jesus restoration was made.

The measure of the love that drove Christ willingly to the cross, and the determination that raised him from the tomb, is beyond the comprehension of the human mind. Our finite minds cannot understand the depth of love, nor the magnitude of the price that was paid on our eternal accounts. Let us thankfully accept it!

Thirty Three

To each soul, there comes a time,
   when it must face itself,
To take an honest look within,
   at what it claims for wealth.
The values we would hold aloft,
   for all the world to see.
Are they the things that stand
   the test for all eternity?
Or do they fall beside the way
   and leave the heart to bleed,
O'er broken dreams and wasted years
   of empty shallow deeds?
The flush of youth so eager spends
   the issues of the soul,
But time will test the choices made,
   the essence of our goal.
And when refining fires of God,
   all dross has burned away,
What then remains shall tell the tale,
   of good or wasted days.
So let us now consider that,
   for which our lives we spend.
Lest we should find our castles tall,
   just ashes in the wind.

The writer of the Word, plainly tells us that each person's life achievements will be tried by fire. When the smoke has cleared, how much of what we have built in our life will still be standing when the true test of real value has been completed? We have only a limited amount of time. Let us be sure we build our lives with eternal materials, lest we stand ashamed midst ashes of a wasted life, on the day of judgment.

Thirty Four

The path of life we walk along,
   so oft described in verse,
Is sung, extolled, and often penned
   by men who are diverse.
The views expressed would speak to us,
   in oh so many ways,
That one might listen long enough,
   from now till end of days.
And what should be the rule to judge
   the rightness of the path?
In fact it seems that every man,
   a different vision hath,
And to which opinion given,
   should I incline my ear?
Should I create a different plan,
   accepting none I hear?
It seems to me, the wiser way,
   is to trust a greater mind,
Ignoring all of mortal thoughts
   and seek God's plan divine.
It comes to me that every man
   is free to choose his own,
But wisdom says the better path,
   would follow God alone.

Opinions are as diverse as the faces we encounter throughout life. It seems everybody has one, but we are reminded of the time in Israel's history when; "Every man did that which was right in his own eyes" the result was chaos, anarchy, and idolatry. The moral status of the world today seems to be the same as it was back then. It seems to encourage each person to act in any manner he chooses. What is needed is a new awakening toward God and his code of morality and righteousness!

Thirty Five

For many, 'tis knowledge, above all they seek,
    and never can their hearts be filled.
More questions than answers in endless array,
    and the fears of the soul never stilled.
For some it is power, their hands would fain grasp,
    yet always 'tis slipping away.
It seems there's no end to the list of the things,
    that men crave, nor the price they will pay.
God's simple truth, when viewed by this world,
    is foolishness, their charges have made.
But those clever ones who scorn at God's Word,
    are snared in the traps that they laid.
And one caught in sin and brought to the fore,
    by skeptics who had much to say;
The words spelled in dust, by the finger of Christ,
    sent her accusers, in shame, all away.

The smugness of those who wrap themselves in their perceived intellectual superiority find themselves confounded by simple truths that pierce to the quick of the soul, when the Spirit of the Holy God uses the dust of the earth to prove his infinite wisdom.

Thirty Six

"In the beginning", the Bible speaks,
　　we would do well to learn,
No other order works in life,
　　I would that all discern;
That every plan should first take note,
　　that God our sovereign is,
And nothing here shall stand the test,
　　unless the plan be his.
Castles, kingdoms, hallowed halls,
　　endeavors of the mind,
Begun and built and turned to dust,
　　with not a trace to find.
Mere mortal men with arrogance
　　and pride have trod the stage,
Then left the scene to fall away,
　　brief notes on history's page.
And when this whirling ball in space,
　　shall burn and pass away,
What will remain of what we've done,
　　this shell just made of clay?
Eternal stands the Word of God,
　　no jot or tittle fade.
And those who cast their fate with him,
　　in beauty all arrayed,
Shall there possess new heavens and
　　new earth, according to his will,
And every promise made by God,
　　unfailingly fulfilled.

Too often we humans fail to stop and realize that before anything
was, God is. When Jesus said, "I am alpha and omega," he wished us to
understand that everything begins and ends in him.

Thirty Seven

Recorded in the sacred book,
    a writer once portrayed,
The wonder of his soul, impressed,
    O'er all the heavens made.
And asked of God in questing mind,
    from deep within his heart,
"What is man, upon this earth,
    that thou so mindful art?"
And yet it speaks to me within,
    midst times of reverie,
The question same; "Oh what am I,
    that he should care for me?"
I look in awe upon this realm,
    the handiwork of God,
And marvel at his love displayed,
    to we, upon this sod.
What drove the one who shaped us all,
    who gave to us his breath,
To take on him a shell of clay,
    to die an outcast's death?
The curse of sin upon the soul,
    the price we could not pay,
Christ paid it all with his own blood,
    to take our sin away.
And I once clothed in rags of sin,
    with shame I now confess,
His grace received, his love has cleansed,
    I'm clad in righteousness.

Without the creating power of God, there would be no magnificent heavens, nor man to ask the question; "What is man?" Compared to God's universe, however, the most amazing act of God is the love beyond measure that drove Christ to the cross on our behalf.

Thirty Eight

There is a way that seemeth right,
    but it would lead astray.
And as it was in garden's ease,
    a serpent points the way.
Beguiling hearts by promise fair,
    of fruits that we might gain.
The simple ones who travel there,
    reap tears, and loss, and pain.
If we should hope, escape to find,
    from snares the tempter lays,
Then daily, with the Word we'll walk,
    and learn his will and ways.
The Word made flesh, came once to dwell
    this earth so full of sin,
Laid down his life on Calvary's cross,
    then, rose to life again.
So now today, no matter where,
    we stop and call his name,
He'll come to us to guide our steps,
    and lift us from our shame,
From all the ways that seemeth right,
    its follies and its loss.
He'll take our guilt, our sin and wrong,
    and nail it to his cross.
And we can walk the higher road,
    the Word to us would send,
Where Jesus will abide with us,
    each day, to be our friend.

Jesus left this world with the promise; "I will never leave you nor forsake you." There is no time or place where Christ will not walk beside us. We never have to face our soul's enemy alone. It is a promise that should bring comfort and peace to each child of God.

Thirty Nine

"Greater deeds than these you'll do",
    was not a promise trite.
Nor were the ones who heard those words,
    men of special might.
Goliath did not fall to earth,
    slain by some magic stone.
The God who walked with David then,
    was not for him alone.
I could remind of furnace hot,
    or speak of lion's dens.
But each and everyone involved,
    were simply mortal men.
There are no secret, magic words,
    or chants that bring about,
Be sure, the walls of Jericho,
    weren't victims of a shout.
The God of all ages, as known
    by those back then,
Can yet today, in this present age,
    still use just common men.
A miracle can come to pass,
    anytime upon this sod,
When one frail child draws near enough,
    to touch the heart of God.

The book of Hebrews reminds us that the great heroes of the Bible, were only ordinary people who tapped into the unlimited power of God. Remember Hebrews 13:8 states; "Jesus Christ the same yesterday, and today, and forever." God's power is available for us today, just as it was back then!

Forty

"He came unto his own, and his own received him not. But as many as received him unto them gave he power to become the sons of God, even to them that believe on his name." John 1:11-12

Called by mercy, surrounded by grace,
    while nothing of worth I could claim,
A sweet gentle Spirit o'er shadowed my heart,
    and ever so soft called my name.
And simply in faith there before him,
    my confession so easily was made.
An unspotted robe I was given,
    with the debt of my sin fully paid.
I rejoice as I think of that moment,
    he cleansed me and called me his son,
And in peace, passing all understanding,
    by God's grace the battle was won.
My heart and all of my being,
    felt the presence of the savior so kind,
In the awe of a soul he thus rescued,
    came assurance, so calm to my mind.
Just a beggar, a tramp, and a rebel,
    no righteousness there could I bring,
Now I stand in his love and his mercy,
    and am called a child of the king.

The very thought of the possibility of being made a son of God, ought to thrill the heart of every sin oppressed child of Adam. The fact that the death of Christ has purchased the means of escape from Satan's control, for each member of our race, is the greatest news the world has ever known.

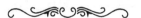

Forty One

"Jesus, keep me near the cross",
    those words so oft we sing,
But do we ever realize,
    what that request might bring?
The cross was once a place of shame,
    a sign of death and pain.
Were I to dwell at Calvary,
    what would my life then gain?
We fain would all, an easier path,
    our heart's desire pursue.
Could it be, as with my Lord,
    a cross awaits me too?
Dare I suppose, no sacrifice,
    to be his child required?
But more than that, is it the way,
    a way to be desired?
For if I hope my soul to rise,
    above this world of strife,
'Tis on a cross, where self must die,
    that I would gain my life.

"For whosoever will save his life shall lose it; and whosoever will lose his life for my sake, shall find it. For what is a man profited if he shall gain the whole world, and lose his own soul? Matthew 16:25-26. Jesus spoke of those who would hoard unto themselves the life they have been given, as being losers in this life, and those who lose themselves in the lives and needs of others, as being the ones who really live. We cannot begin to live as Christians until we have experienced what the Apostle Paul described when he wrote; *"I am crucified with Christ; nevertheless I live; yet not I, but Christ liveth in me." Galatians chapter two.*

Forty Two

The eye of man is never clear,
    when self would hold his gaze.
The view beheld, distorted is,
    as seen through deepest haze.
One's self it seems, to be far worse,
    or else to be too fine.
Oh, would to God, to see ourselves,
    as does the one divine.
An honest view, which adds not to
    the beauty, nor the plain,
That we might learn to work with God,
    his image to obtain.
We often fail when urged to change,
    to see the need so great,
And claim no need within our soul,
    or it might surely wait.
It seems the mind of man, can ne'er
    behold an honest view,
And that is more the reason Lord,
    to leave it up to You.
So teach me now to walk the path,
    that leads me to your goal,
That I might stand, in favor Lord,
    before you right and whole.

We are admonished in God's Word to, "judge not." It seems that when it comes down to judging ourselves, we are never fair. We are either too lenient, or too severe. Let us seek the leading of the Spirit to show us where we need to change. And "lean not to our own understanding." Knowing the will of the Spirit places a greater responsibility upon our determination to seek with the whole heart God's ways, but it will pay off in eternal benefits.

Forty Three

Oh how my heart is thrilled within,
    on calm and balmy days.
And I can speak of fellowship
    with Christ along such ways.
But if I look inside myself,
    and read my mind's deep thoughts,
Can I deny when storms arise,
    I think "Is this what ought
To fall upon my weary soul;
    should I be treated thus?"
And can my eye behold the love,
    that holds me midst the gusts?
So oft I'd walk the pleasant path,
    all strewn with flowers fair,
And would believe that times like these,
    should be the norm, not rare.
But Christ has told the servant here,
    he's not above his Lord,
And I have seen the path he chose,
    as I peruse his Word.
He never shirked to stand the test,
    nor asked to shun the pain,
And I, like him, must bear the cross,
    if I would find the gain.

Many times I have listened to testimonies of professed Christians, who seem to list their material gains above their spiritual progress. I wonder if we of this modern world have lost sight of the admonition to be careful where we allow our heart to become attached. Let us never forget that nothing of this physical world is of any profit to our eternal souls; help us Lord, to keep our eyes on the spiritual achievements and seek to put them first over all else in this world.

Forty Four

"Forsake not the assembling," the apostle once wrote,
    to people so much like we.
It seems in this day, we find more and more,
    who believe, "that is not for me."
I can't comprehend why so many I meet,
    think their lives fit an alternate plan.
They act as if God spoke to everyone else;
    they're exempt from Jesus' command.
How sad for the soul, the results of a life
    lived by; "what's right in my eyes,"
To find much too late, they had been taken in,
    by the master deceiver's bold lies.
I never could fathom, deep in my heart,
    why people treat God like a child.
Picking and choosing what they will obey,
    as if God had no say all the while.
I often question if any would think,
    to behave toward the law of our land,
In the manner they use toward almighty God,
    who holds their soul in his hands?
'Tis sad to admit they don't understand,
    "no shadow of turning with God."
His lesson so clear, "be just, love mercy,
    and walk humbly," here on this sod.

It is sad to say, there are many who presume to tell God what they will, or will not believe about Him and his Word. We must never think we are different and that God will grant us special grace, not available to the average person. Someone stated it clearly, our opinions are not relevant with God, when he penned; "they are not the ten suggestions!"

Forty Five

There are some times, when all alone,
    my savior comes to me,
And speaks sweet peace upon my soul,
    in measures full and free.
And tears well up within my eyes,
    to feel his presence near.
To think that one, yes such as I,
    could be a child that's dear.
That he would stop to take the time,
    to cheer a troubled heart,
And in the battles of this life,
    that he would take my part.
But there contained within the Word.
    a message all might see,
While I was yet a sinner,
    My savior died for me.
What love so grand, amazing grace,
    that drove him to the cross,
That he might pay to ransom us,
    to save our souls from loss.
I am convinced, if this be true,
    his love contains much more,
Than I might speak or even think,
    of all he has in store.
Thus I should never ask of how,
    or why he cares for me,
Just let me Lord, this humble soul,
    surrender all to thee.

That God's love is beyond human expression, it goes without saying. The depth of his blessings are beyond our wildest dreams. Let us rejoice forevermore!

Forty Six

Have you ever stopped to wonder,
   and give yourself to thought,
About a man like Joseph,
   and of the things he sought?
He claims no fame like Mary.
   Who studies o'er his life?
And yet there was a purpose,
   God used him in the strife.
He watched and cared for Jesus
   and Mary through the years,
From Bethlehem, to Egypt,
   and Nazareth, midst his fears.
But few we hear that praise him,
   or talk of all his deeds,
It seems he walked in shadows,
   and none now pay him heed.
He was a man of action
   and faithful to his call,
To take a wife some questioned,
   to be of worth at all.
He fled the wrath of Herod,
   our savior was his trust.
And labored for his family,
   midst the turmoil he was thrust.
There is one thing I'm certain of,
   God used him in his plan,
And I would be well satisfied,
   should I be such a man.

It seems the common desire of most people is to become someone special. But how often do we stop and think just how special some of the common, ordinary, everyday people really are? How many of us wish to fill the shoes of a man like Joseph?

His was an important, but unobserved person in the plan of God.

Forty Seven

Neither prophet, nor poet, I think of myself,
  just one God claims as his own.
I seek not fortune nor fame in this world,
  I'm only on my way home.
But if I can reach down and lift up one heart,
  so broken and trampled by sin,
And point him to Jesus and help him along,
  from a path so dark and so dim.
There's never a calling more worthy to claim,
  than bringing a soul to the light.
Ever and always, surrounded we are,
  by those Satan robbed of their sight.
When asked of my brother; I can't be like Cain,
  turn my back and go my own way.
Many lie bleeding and dying in sin,
  for want of the words we might say.
And where is my neighbor; On Jericho road,
  robbed, and left there to die?
How dare we gather our righteous robes
  about us and then hurry on by?
To a Jew, a Samaritan was worse than a dog,
  if ever a man could ignore,
The needs of a man, who looked down on him,
  who could have had more
Cause to walk by and never look back,
  but with pity he cast down his eyes.
Jesus said to the crowd as he says yet today,
  "we must go; we must do likewise!"

We cannot be the children of God and ignore the casualties of sin lying broken all around us. Yes we are our brother's keeper. The wounded, robbed, dying souls by the wayside are our responsibilities and Christ equates our love for our neighbor as second only to our love for him.

Forty Eight

To every heart, there are the times,
    when shadows seem to creep,
And rob the soul of vision clear,
    with somber thoughts so deep,
To hinder even stauncher saints,
    than you or I might be.
Midst times like these, I tell my soul;
    "to Jesus I must flee."
For Satan like a roaring lion,
    stalks such days and hours,
And searches out which ever one,
    that he, might chance devour.
Draw nigh to God exhorts the Word,
    he will draw nigh to thee,
Resist the devil in the Spirit's power,
    and Satan is forced to flee.
Greater is he, who dwells in us,
    than he who roams this world.
The shield of faith can quench each dart,
    our enemy has hurled.
Yes even midst our darkest days,
    God's light can flood our soul,
And shattered hearts, just by his touch,
    become complete and whole.

The emotional highs and lows, experienced by all of us, can leave us vulnerable to Satan's attacks. We need to realize that human frailties are only proof of our need to walk close beside our savior. May God help us to understand that we will reach perfection only after the resurrection, thus we should not allow the enemy to drag us down when we pass through these dark emotional periods of our lives.

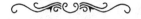

Forty Nine

"Come unto me", the cry of God's heart,
    still rolls o'er the ages of time.
Like sheep gone astray and scattered about,
    what is the answer we find?
No peace for the soul, no hope for the day,
    "vanity," the heart's issued cry.
The shepherd of souls yet seeks out the lost,
    his love would draw us all nigh,
The weak and the worn, the weary of heart,
    to shelter us under his wing.
Sin battered lives, lost dreams and hopes,
    to him all our failures we bring,
He sorts it all out, restoring the soul,
    the song once silenced proclaims.
And being renewed, the old passed away,
    a new creation now reigns.
He calls us to come, to enter his rest,
    his yoke and his burden is light.
We can find shelter inside his fold,
    He will keep watch o'er the night.
There is not a one he will turn away,
    as long as we give him our heart.
The summer's near ended, the day is far spent,
    now is the time; let us start.

The call of Jesus still echoes down through the ages; "Come unto me, and I will give you rest." "He that cometh unto me I will in no wise cast out." Time or situations have not lessened the truth and hope of God's call. It is just as valid now as it was back then. Our hope is still sure and true.

Fifty

"If my people, which are called by my name,
    shall humble themselves, and pray;"
That challenge still echoes around us,
    and calls on our hearts yet today.
To humble our hearts, to turn from our sin,
    forsaking our self centered way,
Our God, in mercy, is waiting to hear,
    and the plagues of this earth he will stay.
Ever and always, like Adam we seek,
    that which appeals to the eye,
And list to the voice that would tell us,
    "ye shall not surely die!"
Oh why give ear to the serpent today,
    ignoring the counsel of God,
And heap to ourselves all the sorrow
    that sin brings to those of this sod.
The lie seems always to draw us,
    the truth, so easily, ignored.
But God in his mercy still beckons,
    "Oh come and be ye restored."
As a father grieves for his children,
    our Savior weeps over the lost,
And laid down his life there at Calvary,
    and lovingly paid all the cost.

It seems that few realize the full ramifications of; "If my people, which are called by my name, shall humble themselves, and pray, and seek my face, and turn from their wicked ways; then will I hear from heaven, and will forgive their sin, and will heal their land." The whole world depends unknowingly on the actions and attitudes of God's people. We need to take serious thought and action as Christians to carry out our obligations.

Fifty One

The angels and host of the heavens,
    given charge to watch o'er men's souls,
Rejoice when one sinner comes to Jesus,
    to be made well and whole.
I am sure all the imps and the demons
    of Satan's unholy throng,
Are weeping and gnashing in anger,
    when the saints sing their victory song.
Should not we who possess here, the kingdom,
    celebrate o'er every new birth?
The price paid in love by our savior,
    tells the world what one soul is worth.
If Jesus could give himself freely
    for the lost and undone of this world,
Should not we who claim his salvation,
    press the battle with banners unfurled?
In this battle there's no place for watching,
    there are only two armies afield,
And each day that passes before us,
    there are countless destinies sealed.
We each must make the decision,
    on which side we will enter the fray,
And many are lost here forever,
    when the choice is made, "Not today."
Would to God we each caught a vision,
    of the impact of actions we take,
And how we might spend our forever,
    regretting an eternal mistake.

There is no middle ground, nor can we be neutral in the struggle between God and Satan's forces. We either serve God or we fight against him, and the stakes are forever.

Fifty Two

When I consider the work of thy hands,
    my heart is stirred deeply within,
And never a doubt remains in my soul,
    of your power to make and to mend.
When darkness covered the face of the deep,
    your Word shaped all I can see.
Where chaos once reigned, you spoke it away,
    leaving beauty and order, so free.
The stoniest places all melted and flowed,
    you shaped and molded with ease.
The rocks and the hills sing forth your praise,
    as well as rivers and trees.
But greater the work you do in the heart,
    all broken and battered by sin,
Where nothing of worth nor beauty was found,
    a life of splendor begins.
Cast away souls with hearts burdened down,
    all ruined and shattered today,
Your grace reaches out, it speaks to the soul,
    and offers us peace for the way.
Your love proved itself at dark Calvary,
    it answered the question for me,
Of why you should care,
    Your creation, your children, set free.

The only answer, to the question of why Jesus died on the cross, is simply; he loved his creation enough to bridge the gap that man through willful disobedience created. His resurrection provided our eternal hope.

Fifty Three

Oh cast your cares upon Jesus,
    he still meets the needs of the heart.
It matters not where you have wandered,
    he welcomes all who would start.
If you should reach out for his mercy,
    his love will envelope your soul.
Then the work of the Spirit within you
    will cleanse and make you whole.
There is nothing his love cannot cover,
    your past forever erased.
Your name inscribed up in Heaven,
    on the door of your mansion is placed.
We know our works cannot save us,
    that price we're unable to pay,
But if we confess and believe him,
    he will walk by our side all the way.
God's love is beyond comprehension,
    our heart, not our head, makes the choice.
Yes ever and always he's listening,
    so today won't you lift up your voice?

A good and caring father seeks to provide happiness and the necessities of life for all his children. He does not consider it a sacrifice to work and plan for their every need. Our Heavenly Father exceeds all our expectations and his love is beyond the scope of the mind of men to fathom.

Fifty Four

Of all the paths that men might take,
   there's one I'd choose, o'er all,
To see beyond the routine things
   and hear the master's call.
To love the Lord with all my heart;
   my neighbor as my life.
To reach a hand, to point the way,
   a shelter in the strife.
But sad to say, this world is full
   of those who scorn God's grace.
They have no time for faith and love,
   they run a different race.
A man might build upon this earth,
   the castles of his dreams.
Immerse himself in untold wealth
   and all the fame it brings.
But what complaint can one man bring?
   "The beggar had no right
To drag himself before my gate,
   I hadn't caused his plight.
I broke no laws, I paid my way,
   so why should I feel shame?"
But in the end, of those two men,
   we know the beggar's name.

What a contrast; the rich man and Lazarus. From the human viewpoint the rich man would be much more important than a rag clad sore infested beggar. The viewpoint of God however, looks at the eternal spirit of a man. While society would look with favor on the rich man and fawn over him, thinking to gain his favor and possibly receive some reward, or monetary gain. In the case of Lazarus, only God saw the sincerity of his heart and judged him worthy of Heaven because of his faith!

Fifty Five

There is a time for everything,
    the writer doeth proclaim,
But not all that we undertake,
    brings glory to God's name.
So many things that come to pass,
    no merit they possess.
Though we can find the time to act,
    is it what God can bless?
So many trivial mundane things,
    in vain they fill our days.
But when accounting for our lives,
    will we regret our ways?
A time to laugh, a time to mourn,
    to break the fallow ground,
All can find the time to act,
    but where might peace be found?
It's not the doing of the thing,
    the sloth spends time, like we.
And we might boast a thousand deeds,
    or only two or three.
But when each one has run the race
    and stands before the King,
'Twill be the motive of the heart,
    when judged in everything.
So never let us on this earth,
    lose sight of time or place,
But spend our days in loving deeds,
    to spread God's love and grace.

Although the writer stated there is a time for everything; he did not intend to infer that all actions in this life are acceptable to God. We must choose carefully how we act, if we would expect God's approval of our lives.

Fifty Six

"Silver and gold, have I none,"
    said Peter at the beautiful gate,
"Such as I have, give I unto thee,"
    to a beggar who could only wait
For someone to share of his wealth that day,
    he hoped for a coin, maybe two,
But, "such as I have", what could that mean?
    How little it was the man knew,
Of the abundance of love, of power untold,
    of grace from our father's throne.
So many needed what Peter could give,
    but the lame man received it alone.
Just looking for treasure, some gold
    he could spend; that which fadeth away,
His hopes must have fallen; what to expect
    from Peter and John that day.
They didn't wait for the man to have faith,
    they lifted him up from the ground,
Stood him on his feet, he leaping with praise,
    was heard by those all around.
But those who claimed to know about God,
    in anger found fault with those men,
Who could offer no money but spoke out for Christ,
    there in the temple again.
They couldn't deny what happened that day,
    they thought to silence the crowd.
But their efforts failed and glory to God,
    the beggar couldn't be cowed.
So let us all learn the lesson God gave,
    with a beggar born crippled for life.
What's impossible with man is no test for God,
    he's greater than all of our strife.

There is no situation on earth that presents a problem for God!

Fifty Seven

"Let not your heart be troubled,"
    the master spoke long ago.
That message rings for all of us,
    who walk this vale of woe.
He did not leave us comfortless,
    his Spirit with us abides,
And through the mazes of this life,
    he wants to be our guide.
This world has nothing such as he,
    to calm the heart of man,
And we have access to God's power,
    when we hold to his hand.
There's not a creature of this earth,
    can steal us from our king,
And what might I desire to ask,
    of him who holds all things.
The race is not unto the swift,
    nor battle to the strong,
In all of these victorious,
    when we to him belong.
So I shall walk this troubled road,
    my prayer to do his will,
For when I cried; "I can't go on;"
    my emptiness he filled.

The brief statement; "I can do all things through Christ which strengtheneth me;" testifies to the truth that God's power is greater than any difficulty we may face in this life. As Christians we need to walk by faith holding fast to all God's promises.

Fifty Eight

With pride I viewed what I had done,
 it seemed a work so grand.
But in a dream quite real that night,
 God sent a reprimand.
It seemed a hand in quiet strokes,
 wrote thus upon my wall;
"Destruction waits for mortal man,
 pride goes before a fall."
How could it be, I erred in life?
 The deed was done, for him.
But when I viewed my motive clear,
 I knew I'd failed again.
'Tis obedience, not sacrifice,
 my Lord desires from me,
A life transformed by God's own Spirit,
 is thus a gift so free.
The essence of mere mortal man,
 so far beneath his king,
Without a touch from Christ's own hand,
 Is devoid of everything,
That lifts the soul to Heaven's heights,
 or fills the heart with song.
No comfort for the wandering soul,
 as it would plod along.
If I would fill my days with deeds
 and words that please my Lord,
I'd seek his will and act in faith,
 ever guided by his Word.

If our lives are not motivated and directed by the love of God, it becomes an exercise in futility. The only works of man that will stand the test of time will be those commissioned by God himself.

Fifty Nine

When I look upon this life,
    so frail and fleeting here.
I question why so many folks,
    ignore what I find dear.
It seems they have no time for God,
    they live a hectic pace,
And give themselves to empty goals
    and spurn a life of grace.
Like lemmings driven to the edge,
    destruction lies in wait,
To claim the masses rushing forth,
    their end, a hopeless fate.
The pride that drives the human heart,
    yields not, to Heaven's call,
But blindly rushes down the path,
    that lures both great and small.
The heart of man so restless lies,
    within the troubled breast.
It never finds its purpose here,
    until in God it rests.
It seeks to hide from its own place,
    in frantic hopeless deeds;
To drown the voice that speaks within,
    of its eternal needs.
But ever faithful to the end,
    God's Spirit probes the soul,
And ever offers till our last breath,
    the grace that makes men whole.

Jesus' love never relents from calling to the lost of this earth. The Holy Spirit never gives up seeking to impress the heart of its need for salvation. The enemy of our soul ever seeks to instill a false sense of peace and security. Remember, everyone needs to make peace with God and allow him to lead them to the judgment without fear.

Sixty

Could I with words a temple build,
    to lift your soul to heights,
Describe to you with vision clear,
    a multitude of sights.
Could I sing praise to thrill the ear
    of things beyond the scope,
Of human thought, of eye or ear,
    and lift the heart with hope,
And should I paint with sweeping stroke,
    of brush in Heavens hues,
To challenge all within the breast,
    of everyone that views.
Could human soul exhaust all forms
    of expression known to man,
I yet would fail to half convey
    the awe that God commands.
My swelling words, my vision bright,
    and praise extolled in song,
Inspiring scenes where masters weep,
    and still 'twould be all wrong.
Our sovereign God, creation fills,
    beyond all time and space.
No human heart, or mind, or eye,
    can encompass his face.
I am convinced there is one thing,
    mere mortals such as we,
Are all required, the scripture says,
    it is *required* of thee,
"To do justly, love mercy,
    to walk humbly with thy God.
This is the task *required* of all,
    each day we walk this sod.

It seems to be easier to stand up and be a martyr; a one time act; than to walk with God daily, consistently, with inspiration and dedication of our heart and will.

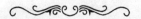

Sixty One

When we look at human life,
    a pattern clear we see.
At every stage and every age,
    desires wrapped up in "me."
It seems to be the way of men,
    from Adam till the end,
Upon ourselves in selfish ways,
    our substance we do spend.
The greatest conflict in each life,
    is fought within the soul,
And self must die in every man,
    before he is made whole.
The enemy arrays himself,
    destruction is his plan,
And heartily affirmed by us,
    and aided by each man.
We plant the seeds and build the walls,
    that trap us in despair.
And then cry out and plead with God,
    that he not leave us there.
The human mind can't comprehend,
    the love that drove our Lord
To sacrifice himself for us
    while we refused his Word.
There is no man upon this earth,
    who might explain God's ways.
But I am certain undying love,
    drew me midst willful days.
And yet some day somewhere ahead,
    known only by my king,
He'll sit me down and take the time,
    to tell me everything.

"For now we see through a glass darkly, but then face to face; now I know in part; but then I shall know even as also I am known." I Cor. 13:12

Sixty Two

There is a gift sent from above,
    to every human heart,
Without beginning or an end,
    where we must make our start.
It truly is the Word of God,
    no scroll could all contain,
Nor could the wisdom of this world,
    attempt to us explain.
It lives today, it always has,
    while eons passed away,
And yet, 'twas given to this world,
    to us, though made of clay.
It draws the child in innocence,
    the sage of countless days.
The heart alone can find its truth,
    the mind cannot explain.
The more we seek to understand,
    the more we must refrain,
From thinking we have found it all,
    its depths of truth no end.
To learn it all, the wisest man,
    eternity would spend,
And still fall short of knowing all
    the essence of our God,
Who lovingly would walk with us
    each day upon this sod.
And thus throughout all of my life,
    I'll gladly study him,
Until his call shall bring me home,
    where then I shall begin.

I would, like Mary, seek that good part of sitting at the feet of Jesus, not being denied the privilege of learning of him.

Sixty Three

"My strength is made perfect in weakness,"
    the Apostle so plainly was told,
And he admonished his converts,
    at the throne of God's grace, "Come bold."
We know we're beset by an army,
    whose leader hates all things of God,
And we, in the midst of this battle,
    fight powers not derived from this sod.
The weapons we use are not carnal,
    they come from the heavenly realm.
Our leader, the King of creation,
    victoriously stands at the helm.
The foe is massed all around us,
    and they think by their numbers they'll win.
But greater is he that's within us,
    than the one who leads armies of sin.
And though the battle grows hotter,
    in God's Word his promise to saints,
The wings of eagles he gives us,
    though we're weary, we walk and not faint.
Yes, one day the war will be over,
    we'll see Jesus our master and King,
In that great banquet hall up in Heaven,
    the song of our victory will ring.
And there, forever eternal, in his presence
    we shall sing with the throng
Of the angels and hosts of the heavens,
    that glorious and wonderful song
Of praise to the great God eternal,
    the omnipotent, the Holy, I Am.
And casting our crowns all before him,
    sing "Worthy yes Worthy, The Lamb!"

On that day when the fulfillment of all God's plans for humanity comes to pass, we will join our voices with the host of Heaven, praising our wonderful magnificent God.

It is my prayer that the readers, of this that God has brought forth from my heart, might receive an inspiration and vision that assists them in their everyday lives for as long as they shall live.

I confess that I have only been the vehicle through which God has produced this collection of poems. I hope you might be as blessed when reading and pondering the messages they bring as I have been while composing them.

God bless you is my prayer

-Michael Grebe

CPSIA information can be obtained
at www.ICGtesting.com
Printed in the USA
LVHW091411271020
669945LV00007B/263

9 781479 782567